THE RADIO ROOM

Also by Cilla McQueen
Homing In (1982)
Anti Gravity (1984)
Wild Sweets (1986)
Benzina (1988)
Berlin Diary (1990)
Crikey (1993)
Markings (2000)
Axis (2001)
Soundings (2002)
Fire-penny (2005)
A Wind Harp (CD, 2006)

THE RADIO ROOM

Cilla McQueen

OTAGO

Published by Otago University Press,
Level 1 / 398 Cumberland Street,
PO Box 56, Dunedin, New Zealand
Email: university.press@otago.ac.nz,
Fax: 64 3 479 8385

First published 2010
Copyright © Cilla McQueen 2010
ISBN 978 1 877578 03 8

Written and published with the
assistance of Creative New Zealand

Publisher: Wendy Harrex
Designer: Fiona Moffat
Author photograph: Isabella Harrex
Printed in Aotearoa New Zealand
by Printlink Ltd, Wellington

POEMS

To Andrea

A GHOSTLY BEAST

We scared ourselves white in the bothy
the night that one of us expressed the prideful wish
to dine on Clanranald's finest beast.

Then came a lowing above the song of the storm,
a lowing so close, if you could see through stone
it would be just outside the wall!

We talked ourselves to sleep that night,
blocked our ears to the tempest roiling,
talked ourselves out of it –

But when the first ignorant ventured at dawn
outside, he found the encircling hoofprints –
proof, in the very fabric of the island.

OUR COW

By salt, by fire and water
secured from enchantment,
our cow is in the meadow,

Beside the fertile patch of ground left fallow,
sacred to that deity, whose name is lost.

ABOUT THE FOG

Damp sea-fog lay like a sheep on my journal
outside all night on the table,
turned radiant blue ink to turquoise wash
through which the permanent horizons stared
twenty-eight pages empty.
                Of vanished thoughts here
and there word-slivers, blots in the gutter, bled edges;
some legible sentences in ballpoint.

As if by tears
            lost the death of my mother,
the reunion with my tokotoko at Matahiwi,
Orepuki Hopupu ho nengenenge matangi rau
at hand beside me now, ribboned, knotty, sleek,

Washed away, goes without saying, language
absorbed by a fog to dissolve in the sun.

ALTAR (ELEMENTS 1)

One rock, another rock,
a flat rock on top.

On this we laid our sin, the Great Auk
that we killed for fear of sorcery

Our sin because
she was the last bird of her kind.

Here the Amazon once laid
a pair of antlers and a bowl of oil

In thanks to the Being
for new life, another year.

On this I laid my prayer,
a woollen thread and a button.

BEACON (ELEMENTS 2)

Discovered in lenses,
bent around stars.

I leap island to island,
altar to altar.

Breathe life into things,
one word to another,

Sweep the night seas
with a quartz shiver.

My feet of quicksilver
dancing on water.

BOOKWORM

Been here in arms, fresh linen,
before snow's aery characters
illuminated, drifting
down darkness beyond a window
here before –
tell past to know time present
past familiar, dawn cloud lifting
from a dreaming mountain.
Hold the image against meeting,
knowing time and place
coincidence, gaudeamus
in the next dimension,
life history, manifold instant
of a given point.
At this juncture,
memory scrolling time, I
who I am drill like a bookworm
leaves tunnels perfectly aligned leaves
as a closed book,
memory keeping
portholes in cliff emplacement
blast chamber tunnels, open to shock,
delight; in arms, fresh linen held up
secure, newborn
in fresh white sleeves
and this remember not
but have been told she said
she has been here before
and shown at last
snow's aery characters
white on black,
on dark ground, white words
and white ground dark words:
'Writing was most astonishing to them;
they cannot conceive how it is possible

for any mortal to express the conceptions
of his mind in such black characters
upon white paper.'

(Martin Martin, 1716, of the inhabitants of St Kilda)

Foveaux   Cilla '10

COASTLINE (ELEMENTS 3)

I meet myself
coming the other way.

Distinguish between
two grains of sand.

No power on earth can change me,
nothing pins me down.

Within my high and low
I belong to none,

A sacred slate
where law is written.

CRAZY HORSE

Thanks for the dream of the sapphire sea last night,
ultramarine-speed ocean framed by rocks, so bright it sang.

Harmonically, I send pearls rolling down cabbage leaves,
diamonds from my washing line, bronze totara,
the harbour's violet pewter plate in this fine dusk.

All day the sapphire sea and the words have held my eyes.
As promised now and then a message comes of startling loveliness.

CUP OF TEA

My mother's sugar bowl
is tinged with sadness

And cannot be put
together again.

Tea of tar and smoke. Tea of green.

A china bell, a silver spoon,
whirl a pool, lip a fine warm rim.

Smile over it.

A place to rest,
a small vessel decorated with roses.

ETCHING

Art ages.
For instance, this view of York Minster engraved with a fine burin.

In the foreground an upright car of 1930s' vintage with a cloth top, square back window, bumpers and narrow wheels is either parked or driving towards the cathedral through deep shade cast by a tall tree on the left. The shadow stretches across the road almost to the centre of the picture.

On the right-hand footpath, opposite the reaching shadow, a single figure walks beside a fence towards the cathedral. In the middle distance four people stand to the right of the entrance. Further reduced by distance, a group of three on the steps in front of the door.

The distant three are little more than scratches but it is possible to see from the arrangement of their lines that a tall man, hands clasped behind his back, his legs two fine strokes, is bending slightly towards the woman beside him who is middle-aged, well-dressed, with a pale fur around her shoulders. Fox. Standing beside the woman is a gauche, slim-shouldered girl.

The engraving of light areas is so feathery that the outline of York Minster is faintly blurred. Shaded areas are hatched. The cathedral is bathed in sunlight from high on the left. It might be spring, late morning, after Matins.

Of the group on the right, two are children. A boy of about eight wearing a cap, hands in his pockets, stands near his smaller sister. With the use of a magnifying glass one can see that their mother is wearing a knee-length chequered skirt, a fitted jacket and a beret. The other figure might be a woman with her back turned, wearing a fur coat over a dark skirt below the knee.

The single figure on the right is unlike the groups outside the church, whose shadows are miniatures of the larger shadow's strong horizontal. This figure is going in the direction of the Minster but is perhaps about to turn the corner of the garden and walk away down the western side.

A scarf over her hair, she walks heavily, bent slightly forwards under the weight of a sack on her back. Her gait seems measured, trudging.

The dark streak of shadow across the base of the towers draws the eye which then travels up to their filigree crenellations. A difference in the line distinguishes the laden figure in the foreground from the groups near the cathedral steps.

On the left-hand footpath near the car, opposite the woman going the other way, three other figures can be seen in the shadow of the tree.

There is energy in the lines of all but the woman who is walking towards the church but not going to church. She is perhaps on her way home with a bag of washing. Head bent, she leans slightly to the left because of what is slung over her right shoulder. She walks past four rounded trees, fruit trees perhaps, half the height of the tree across the road which casts the long shadow. The shade of the small trees is diffuse.

York Minster is bathed in light. The yellowed etching is in its original mount and lacquered frame. The signature at bottom left, in pencil. The top stroke of the 'J' carries on to the end of the signature, paralleled by a confident underline, the hand light, rounded. The middle name of the artist is hard to read; it looks like Alphege, or Alphye. On the right side of the etching is a sepia dot. Foxed.

FOVEAUX EXPRESS

Diesel sounds aromatic
magenta, oxblood,
mineral smooth
any how as boronia

Swivel that levers
a shoepolish lid,
key curls oily metal.
Poetry takes you apart,

Puts you back different
as this day's passage
on shapeshifting water,
one to another island

Swift as the stroke
of a pen the toothed strait
on the whale's path
chewed through, islets

Scattered between,
text in motion
gimballed on muscling
swells, word–ware, cargo.

FUGUE, 1892

From the Zealandia Hall on Esk Street,
her oilskin craft fiercely inflated

with hot smoke from a fire in a tin-roofed trench
by the method invented by Daring Donald MacDonald,

manuka-scented Miss Viola rises
like Monsieur Charles on lift-off from the Tuileries

in the Moment of Universal Hilarity,
epiphany of antigravity.

She soars aloft two hundred feet,
alas not high enough to use the parachute,

before a cold Antarctic airstream sinks her down
amid the giant fuming folds of her balloon,

zeal tempered by experience,
before the Temperance Hall, also on Esk.

IN HAND

Poem in hand,
the tendons slide and muscles
smile under the skin.

A shoulder-twitch
sends nectar down the arm,
the scurrying point encrypts

Rillets, clicks, warbles;
in a kowhai two bellbirds
sing upside-down

Their green glass song
as raindrops blur these lines,
the meantime handwritten.

LENS

Rinso.
Soap-scum in the concrete tub,
brass plug, brass chain.
Webbed wash-house window
soap sliver sunlight
dusty dwang, bee-sting blue-bag
green steel drum agitator
washing machine.
Mangle feed sheets flat
deep water cold to elbows,
red hands, through and again,
too thick the mangle bangs apart.
A wicker washing basket.

At the workbench
he in school uniform
grinding for hours a disc of porthole glass
wave-green inside, concave with carborundum;
peers at the lens
telling of quasars, pulsars, light-years,
imaginary numbers,
launches into infinity
with the same confident science that asserted
when he was four and I was three,
and I believed,
the correct name for a small electricity substation
to be 'Abensikinsaw.'
(a-b-e-n-s-i-k-i-n-s-a-w)

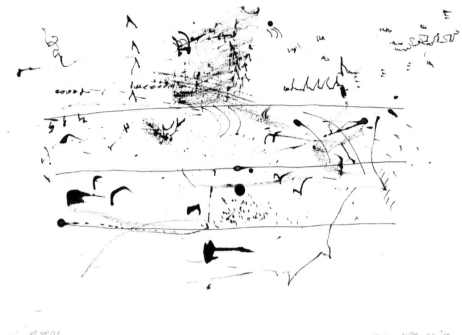

BIRDS

(signature) '10

LETTER TO HONE 1

Dear Hone, by your Matua Tokotoko
sacred in my awkward arms,
its cool black mocking
my shallow grasp

I was
utterly blown away.

I am sitting beside you at Kaka Point
in an armchair with chrome arm-rests
very close to the stove.

You smile at me,
look back at the flames,
add a couple of logs,
take my hand in your bronze one,
doze awhile;

Open your bright dark eyes,
give precise instructions as to the location of the whisky
    bottle
on the kitchen shelf, and of two glasses.

I bring them like a lamb.
You pour a mighty dram.

MINING LAMENT

I went to see the golden hill
but it had all been mined away
all that's left is an empty bowl
of yellow gorse and rutted clay

But it had all been mined away
except a clay bluff topped with stone
in yellow gorse and rutted clay
one stubborn relic stands alone

Only a clay bluff tipped with stone
remains of the hill the painter saw
one stubborn relic stands alone
of a rounded hill of golden ore

Remains of the hill the painter saw
rutted clay and a stumbling stream
a rounded hill of golden ore
sluiced away with a sluicing gun

Rutted clay and a stumbling stream
all that's left is an empty bowl
sluiced away with a sluicing gun
I went to see the golden hill

(after a painting by Christopher Aubrey, c. 1870)

BIRDS

Cora McEwen '10

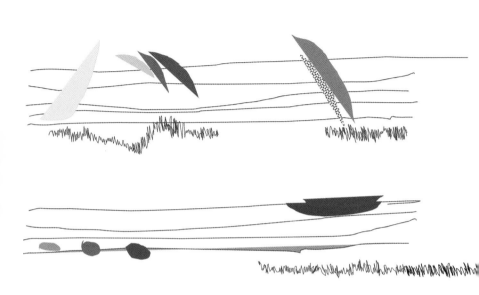

NOTES FOR MOTHS

The music is extremely quiet and may as well be played
mentally in silence.

The sounds are the slight brushes and bumps of moths
against a pane of glass.

The glass divides violins drawing bowed notes, firstly in
a primrose choir and secondly in a trio of peach, lavender
and cranberry, from what lies below these events: a slight
scratching, as delicate as a burin etching, varying pitch as
low as can be heard.

As usual a period of silence or an angel passing over.

The scratching or cross-hatching is resumed by the
blackcurrant violin, evenly.

Meanwhile a spotted shag and a grey heron dive one after
the other for the same fish.

Three round steps from pale lilac to plum, a very slight declension.

The lilac barely fades and resumes where umber and
mauve clouds gather.

The thrumming becomes insistent and ends with emphasis.

PASSION PANTOUM

Getting along like a house on fire
playing around like a couple of kids
fanning the flames of wild desire
head over heels and flipping our lids

Playing around like a couple of kids
speeding about like killer whales
head over heels and flipping our lids
fast and close as a fish with two tails

Speeding about like killer whales
a spooning pair in a blue lagoon
fast and close as a fish with two tails
kissing romantically under the moon

A spooning pair in a blue lagoon
(for you have caught me fair and true)
kissing romantically under the moon
(subliminal background digeridoo)

For you have caught me fair and true,
getting along like a house on fire
(subliminal background digeridoo)
fanning the flames of wild desire

PHOTON

If I stay here
long enough,
if black holes empty
the corruption
of the universe
into a lake of light
that leaches
incoming to me
stippled through
some permeable skin
between that timeless
place and this
where I sit
on an upturned apple box
in the shade of my hat
looking up
through the pores
of its straw,
might I tell
singularity
from manifold,
one luminous emissary
pure of purpose,
a newborn
photon?

POEM

Poem a poem
the inside poem
the words other in
inside drawn eyeless
toe to top fingered
light, gnostic
valiant, innocent
fruit and rind.

Rind and fruit,
innocent, valiant,
gnostic. Light
fingered top to toe,
eyeless drawn inside
in other words the
poem inside the
poem a poem.

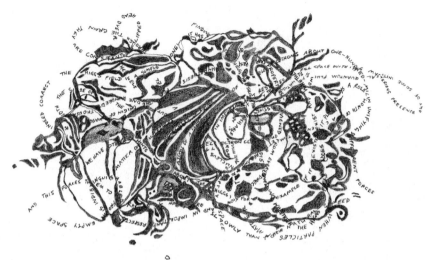

HIGGS. A HYPOTHESISED PARTICLE   Charles Oliver '09

PRIVATE VIEW

The hawthorn twigs knobbled with buds.
A spiderline anchored to the farthest twig of the branch above me
slopes down seven feet to the lowest twig on the trunk.

Webs and guy-ropes everywhere, sliding gleams.
You'd have to jump from the top twig, spinnerets working like mad,
in a stiff easterly, to swing that far.

Out of a hole pokes the pointed head of a grub.
At eye-level with the ground I see its round black nose,
soft pea-green skin and sparkling eyes.

Its forelegs wave as the body squeezes out, reaching to the light,
stops half-way and flops on its side to bask in the sun, at ease.
I am too big to be seen, like the weather.

INCORPORATING THE OYSTER (1)

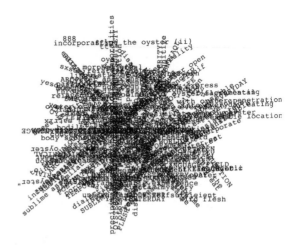

incorporating the oyster (ii) Erica McKenzie '09

RED HERRINGS

Scribe a surface with a nib.
Represent in words a circle.

Inscribe (a geometric construction) inside (another construction)
so that the two are in contact but do not intersect.

Describe a membrane of supersymmetrical elementary particles.

Circumscribe a geometric construction around another construction
so that the two are in contact but do not intersect.

Ascribe beauty to truth.

REPRISE

Who are we now, who were we anyway?
Hard put to say, but not the same as she
imagined five-and-twenty years ago,
lazing on schist at Frankton, looking down
at Wakatipu in translucent scales
descend from jade to alizarin violet
lake, rippled by rising trout in perfect
circles, writing how it was to live
in Aotearoa's Otago,
in halcyon days before the didymo,
before the population rose above
four million and the houses spread across
the Frankton flats and down the Frankton arm
to Kelvin Grove. I thought I saw, last time
revisiting, the skinny, bushy spike
of lancewood that I planted on the dusty
hillside near the path down to the silver
gravel crescent beach below, contoured
by changes in the level of the lake.
At night our fire might catch an eel, with sweet
white fine-boned flesh inside the fat and leather
mucous skin, to eat. Où sont, enfin,
les neiges d'antan? Rosehips, wild thyme, tussock,
bracken? Tadpoles in jam-jars, basking skinks
on baking rocks, green frogs and dragonflies
glittering in rushes in the pond, where now
'Grande Vue' and 'Bella Vista' vie ensconced
in asphalt streets for views of mountain snow?
Who rules the hinterland but overseas
investors, mark the ones who bought the middle
of the map for haven safer than
'back home.' Who's bent on gold in seams beneath
the weathered land at Ohai, Omakau,
Macraes'? Coal, lignite, gas and oil – not we
who love wild places, virgin terrain, pristine

and unharmed – though some love only Peter
Jackson's, that are shown in Hollywood –
but corporate bodies with undreamed-of cash
to buy up land and wait until some pesky
Act's repealed, then rape? The land lies passive
under damming, excavation, human
habitation, subdivision, pylons,
pipelines, sewage ponds and cow-piss, in
a different time-scale from the humans who
exploit her attributes – and patient to
a fault – that's doomed to shift, perhaps, one day
and bring things to a swift conclusion. We
may foul our nest who open up the country
like a frontier – subdivision creeping
up the flanks of the Remarkables –
and next it's Kingston or Glenorchy – fix
the roads and there's another way to make
the landscape pay for being itself. Busloads
of tourists gaze with awe, buy souvenirs,
eat, text and pee, depart with photographs.
The feisty Kawarau escapes the lake
through gates and plunges free as horses down
the gorge to meet the Clutha at the rocky
junction where their waters used to run
at Cromwell, turquoise into cobalt blue.
That's drowned in Dunstan now, an older story
fading as we speak – not in the blunted
language of the internet, but with
the poetry that calls through space to pierce
the insulation of complacency
that wraps the land and our naivety,
whose burning need for electricity
exposes us to foreign exploitation.
When I return to homing in, to dance
on the meniscus of another lake –
Mahinerangi – early morning, when
the glassy water held our weight in light –

she grieves. Wind-farming mooted, shall we never
see again her velvet Lammerlaws
unpricked by corporate voodoo pins, unlaced
with power lines? Sowing the upland air
with mills may reap a whirlwind, presently.
The talk is as a balance sheet; narcissi
contemplate reflections mirrored in
a boardroom table, reconciling beauty's
loss with gain, their view unchanged since the
industrial revolution. Poets awake!
who mine the labyrinth of poetry
for gems of sonnet, ode and threnody,
while losing contact with reality –
the natural landscape facing quick extinction.

RIPPLES

The computer is dead; long live the computer.
In the meantime I write by hand.

Across the road has appeared a For Sale sign
in long grass beside the toetoe in the empty section.
In the middle distance, wind-burned iron roofs chafed by macrocarpa,
wooden power poles, manuka, the Challenge garage,
cars on the bridge
to the island harbour, containers, cranes, warehouses,
fishing boats, ships.

Stockpiled woodchips, tawny forests piled like salt.
Moon-grey sheep-fold in a stony pasture.
The far shore underlines blue mountains.
Across the harbour against the sinuous ranges
stands a white and grey Lego block,
the new milk powder plant, fifteen minutes on the arc by road
from here to there. When my eyes sweep the horizon
they come across a Lego block where there was none.

In the slow ground boulders grow.
Silvered timbers fold the sheep.
Cloud cliffs over Konini, five miles high from west to east.
Agate pebble in my palm
feels like rhyme to my warm skin.
Five dimensions coiled inside, colour deepened by my tongue.

I see Hone with clarity.
The bronze sheen of his skin,
tapering fingers, hand on my arm.
He might be just up the road at Kaka Point.

Alone within alone.
Petrified whalebone.

Tui twangs, triggers ripples.
Under the wilding branches magnified sepia leaf-shadows
play on viridian mosses, rusty iron, ferns, rotten logs.
Pile dead branches and jump on them.
In shade and shattered light dull logs crack, twigs snap.
Floored with leaf-mould, fern, deep loam, this is the hut.

In koromiko shade an iridescent diagram,
fine landing strip, concentric trap,
text between twigs, arachnid syntax,
parlour game in a gossamer field
of forty radii, seven anchors, three strong horizontals.
Along these lines slide spectral parallactic gleams.

I fell in the window. He was asleep in front of the potbelly.
Deaf smile, shining-eyed surprise –
I was afraid you might have burned your legs.
After the funeral service you leaned down towards me out of a cloud;
'Kia mau!' you shouted into my mind.

You might be talking with Joanna.
There she is in a red coat arriving on the ferry.
I watch her painting watercolours. Colours bless the paper.
'A shape to part the space,' she smiles, 'Morandi.'
Quietly, she is gone.

Dawn or dusk? I can't quite hear what they are saying,
I can't get a handle on them, they pull away like water.
Swirling kelp wind, cabbage trees green-faced wildcats.
The house bangs like a cardboard box.
It's calm in here.
Some shells empty, some shells full.
My friends talking quietly, just out of ear-shot.

Mist fills the harbour.
Only the tip of the smelter chimney is showing,
a black accidental on white. The long wharf juts hatched across
nothing.
Straight lines and clustered blocks, taupe, beige, aluminium,
blend with the sand, sea, isabelline sky.

I was astral travelling.
Set in the middle knuckle of his hand
a round World, deep blue and green, a jewel,
a navigation device.
He stretched his arm and we flew beyond the Last Scattering,
beyond the primal molecules
where Nothing warps at the approach of light.

Soul wrapped in a mystery.

Don't worry, when the planet is completely wrecked

the seas will deepen for a time until they disappear in mist
and we are left like Mars.
The last of us might carve some mighty lines in Earth
like Nazcar lines – or Boreray – scrape off the turf
to leave a message on the hill, visible from Hirta –
great navigation lines that point through space
to join with other lines,
our landing strips on some green other world.

There is no malice in the computer,
nor inclination towards good.
In language ether particles form;
word behaviours give thought tongue
in codes and keys –

Then there is an earthquake.
The kitchen cupboards judder as if a tractor drove across the roof
windows struggling panes/ what if/ disrupted/ the cupboards

tumbled/ the piles
collapsed/ the tidal wave impending/ giant broccoli/ without
malice/ keys and codes in tongue
Certainly uncaring. I need Bell tea, for Earl Grey is insipid.
In the kitchen hot teabag juice through fingers,
dropped in the sink a dry bud.

Cosmic code winks on power lines after the billions of rain.
Legs piston past on the white Staffy, Oscar.

Bidibids, snags, pulled threads,
flaws in the weave, points de repère.
Can't be sure of molecules making us up momently
whose memory expands with time
and over time the mind
caught on a detail, thorn, spark, madeleine, opening
a bubble
torus
wormhole;
via chance harmonics,
pools of connection, shocks and ripples,
traversing dimensions.

A shape to part the space –

The edges are shy and to be approached with caution
lest they lose their inner concentration, become self-conscious
in the Adam-and-Eve effect
slip through a gap, perhaps,
change phase – subject to object,
innocence to experience, perhaps.

So   turn stone
        over
                    on the tongue.
★

SOAPY WATER

Despite the recession
it is unlikely that poetry prices will rise.
Poetry produces unreliable returns.
Alternative poetries are looking interesting.
You are urged to conserve and not to waste a drop.
For instance, replace a tap that dripped and dripped with a
    dripping tap,
or you may even choose to rewrite, eliminating the phrase entirely.

Please do not let it run for ages while you look out the window,
testing it with your hand until it is as hot as you really like it.

Never leave a working poem unattended.
Turn off a poem when it is not successful
Much can be recycled, the new on the bones of the old.
Expressive efficiency can be improved by radiation and convection;
please avoid fumes and combustible release of trapped gases;
burning poetry gives only momentary satisfaction.

A cheaper poem can be as efficient if not as attractive.
Try installing a poetry pump.
(New poetry is slimline and often puzzling)

World poetry is running low. Naturally, there is speculation
in solar poetry, wind poetry, tidal poetry,
all as old as mankind, since he learned to talk to himself.
Turn poetry off at the wall to avoid leakage.
Careless poetry is potentially hazardous.
Do you have a poetry guard?
Are you sure you are using dry poetry?
Knock it and listen.

You take Risk if it has been dislodged, ill-maintained, overloaded,
you may cause Flash when operated. Such as this.
Please have it repaired by a competent Poet.

Ensure poem is in a suitable container.
Unexpected poems must be safely housed,
as some remain active long afterwards.
(You can test your poem in soapy water)

TALKING TO MY TOKOTOKO

You came from the river-mouth near Orepuki
in a flash-flood timber tangle.
Stu pulled you out, pleased by your straightness where it mattered,
detail where it mattered.
Serpentine river-rakau
waiting at Matahiwi.

★

Ripped out after the mountain-shaker
tangled roots and branches swept together
woven in a basket-dam.
Another storm, high tide will suck the blockage out.

Let go the roots when a laughing man
leaps up on top and pulls out of the kete
an idiosyncratic stick with attitude;
jumping down says, For you, my dear, to me,
whangai child drawn from a tangle of time
home to Murihiku.

★

Poetry listens, speaks to the heart.
River-weft orisons.
I'll come and fetch you, rakau.
We'll travel home together.
I miss your stern sinew.

★

Dusk late sun cabbage tree windshorn westerly
skirt of gleaming leaves around her supple trunk
another like a collar at the division of her branches
two outer branches curving up like arms, each waving leaves in
    bunches
two inner branches round her head, a spiky quivering crown.

Dancing tree, spirit and rhythm of wood,
I look forward to your company.
Your bird's-neck-shaped twist
where my hand will rest.

★

My right-brain wrist is in a splint.
Glass dribble blistering rainy distortions.
Equality of birth and death.
No one without the other.
Today I have news that my mother may pass away within a week.

Eight white Spoonbills fishing in a tidal pool.

★

I came to Matahiwi, crying for her.
I heard your Maori name
and said your Maori name.
Westerly wind on the slopes of Motupohue –
is that it, Orepuki Hopupu ho nengenenge matangi rau?
Ghosts from an enchanter fleeing?

When I touched your satin grain,
the hundred rippling words of poetry,
heron's head casqued with beaten metal,
ferrule linked by sky-blue to Michele,
my knowing hands remembered your landscape,
where to place my thumb
and rest my wrist on the grain of your heron-neck,
graced with a fine muka plait.

THE HOLE

Measure a black thread.
Roll one end between forefinger and ball of thumb
to a small knot tangle.
Thread the other, moistened by lips to a point,
through the eye of the needle.
Consider the hole in the heel.
Engage with the sock.
Mercury's wing would fit.
There is no ironic distance between us, Sock,
for I must remove my glasses
to obtain a microscopic view
of you.
            Is what I perceive as a void,
such as the void in Eridanus that intrigues me,
so from your viewpoint? Do you know
that you have nothing in you –
an unravelling place,
a shirking, Sock, of the looping continuous
cause that defined you, shaped your ideal,
but for the hole,
the void wherein there is no matter, not a skerrick?
I'd like to go to Eridanus when I die.
Meanwhile, darn it,
the steel tip needling in and out
between there and not-there, defines
edge where there was none, fell whereon
the latticework will be attached,
                                    as is,
between the gutter and the house,
tautened the pragmatic architecture of spiders.

THREE ELABORATIONS

1

Beside the reservoir the flax flowers flame
in curving pods, on shining stems like long
dark hair. You make a boat of stems, a green
sail of a blade, and send it chiselling
through clouds in peat-bronze water. In the heart
of flax, a mordant resin fixes time.
By Foveaux Strait, where endless kelp recoils
and coils again, I hear the ocean's pulse.
The rip is cracking at the harbour heads,
the huia feathers of an ancient house.
I won't find you around these rocks and paths
tonight, nor at the Eagle, Age nor Club –
you've gone with Ganymede, beloved one,
to fill the crystal glasses of the gods.

2

A sycamore seed, a gull allows the wind
to lift her clear beyond the shoulder of the hill.
The macrocarpa brawl and boil,
a flagpole bears a guttering blue flame.
Once, as we walked the spiral summit path,
you swore to send a message back from death –
if any sort of language could be found,
if any metaphor could pass in dream
between that world and this – I'll never know
if it was you who turned that sandy beach
to palimpsest, whereon a pointed stick
described a spiral, from the other side,
or if you sent the sapphires, set like flowers,
whose smallest, darkest stone was named The Eye.

3

Or were the sapphires conjured up by mirror
neurones crystallising memory,
that small stone named for 'I be watchin' ee!'
The fishermen who crowded in to warm
their hands at the coal range, the copper water
cylinder galumphing as it boiled,
the downdraught puffing smoke into the room
until the air was blue and eyes were red,
the weather's fury drowned by laughter, clinking
glasses, empty VB bottles queueing
by the sink – all gone – the house as quiet
as Miss McKenzie's old piano – swept
into the past, like sea-foam in a wake,
except for my own eyes that witnessed it.

TIME (ELEMENTS 4)

I am and again
out of myself
catch me
waiting for no one

Taking my own
out of mind
once upon one I and
tide attend none

Between self
and signature
beyond number
mark my measure.

TO A BABY

A banquet in a crust of bread,
a bright fire in a piece of coal,
a coin to buy the things you need;
these tokens in a scallop shell.

A bright fire in a piece of coal,
the simple gifts of food and warmth,
these tokens in a scallop shell
will bless your table and your hearth.

The simple gifts of food and warmth,
a crust of bread, a silver coin,
will bless your table and your hearth
and make a warm and happy home.

A crust of bread, a silver coin,
a piece of coal to light your fire
and make a warm and happy home
will bring you all that you desire.

A piece of coal to light your fire,
a coin to buy the things you need,
will bring you all that you desire,
a banquet in a crust of bread.

UMBRELLA

Irregularities in early space multiplying gave birth to variety in all
things in luminous thought-fields.
Soft pink new potato skin to my lips, five identical peas in a pod
nuzzled like bumblebees a scented lily. Gold pollen on my nose
all morning.
The sun umbrella leans against a tree. Striped blue yellow and
white canvas with a ragged grey fringe, rusted metal pole,
soon it'll go to the tip. It is a relic, umbrella of my childhood,
attached to me for decades, too rusty to put up, canvas rotten,
history known only to me here under this tree.
A whole life history will disappear when I die or forget it.
It has certainly existed for a period –
if not, lack must unravel through my life like a run in a stocking.
Wakatipu glittering, I'd be on the step, doors held open by brass
hooks. Hot schist slabs underfoot; through bracken and rosehip
down the track to the gravel beach.
We drove with Dad to the garage in Frankton, balancing the wire
handle of the billy on our knuckles so as not to slop the milk. Full stop.
Blue meniscus in the bottle. Clean the reservoir,
eject blue-black whorls, gossip in clear water, fill the pen.
Feathered golden arrow down the milled steel barrel to the nib.
Miles of molecules lined up in knotted and sinuous inky roads
carry. When I write in my mind about this umbrella
I feel the movement of the nib make the words as I'm thinking,
phantom fingers guide the curlicues, silky surfaced nerve-ends.
Thistledown, a point of light. Gaps and slips in time,
a current – eddies, breeze coming up – tide change,
fishing boats heading home.

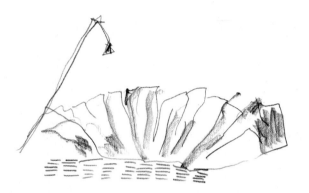

CRANE & PINE-CHIP PILE, BLUFF

WASH

In a Warwick 1B8 A4
I log the days, trail words around the house,
inside, outside, up the back under the trees.
We were six weeks into J12/10.

This morning when I opened the curtains
the window was a blank
white sheet, all sound damped by nuzzling fog.

I wanted to write about the Kotuku,
lost in the Strait four years ago.
Every year at muttonbird-time
I remember the texture of my friend's long hair.

Hone, if you were alive right now I'd roast a few fresh birds and
bring some oysters up the road to Kaka Point. And a bottle of
Te Mata wine. Have you tried Zara?

The pen was missing too –
they'll be together somewhere in the house or outside
on the table, last night stargazing, too cold, morning fog, O my
dear written pages washed-out turquoise mush –

Peel apart   damp translucent skins   fragile   very old person

nerve   shadows   permeate   sparing   grace this year

ends of   right as rain there   our   translation and thin

*   season   either   go sorrow   bruise   through   all that*

*   texture of muttonbird-time*

*   vanished intimacies*

WINDOW

Steam train across the sky
in white puffs even
no edge to their alphabet, vaporous islands
shifting of coastline, deceptively
soft-looking, heavy with water
above the aery metal harbour.
The golden profiles of the woodchip
stockpiles awaiting relief
increasing daily, gaunt Alps.

When the ship comes in
the forests will flow along the conveyor belt,
shapeshift into a wooden pod.

A crane leans over a tawny pyramid,
tip above apex.
An inverted triangle of blue water
balances between greater and lesser
stockpiles, point on the wharf,
base the far shore where blue hills parallel
diaphanous triangular snowcaps, Takitimu.
Imaginary reflection above,
a pyramid of light.

The whole sky pale and bare
but for one lenticular cloud,
head of a kotuku gliding in from the west.

WOODCHIPS

29.3.09
Celia McKeever

YNYS ELEN

Imagining Ynys Elen, ancestral island,
I step ashore on a green leaf edged with foam,
a rocky landing at the stem. Three miles long,
half a mile wide. The white track hugs the cliff.
It's steep. Rest half-way up the zig-zag
in a patch of shade. There are no trees.

The road leads past the church and farmhouse,
through the farmyard and continues over moors
dotted with old stones standing and fallen,
past Quarter-mile, Half-mile, Three-Quarter-Mile
to the northern tip where the Virgin's Well
pours fresh water into salt.

Church, farm, castle, lighthouse, graveyard.
Low rumble, seabirds, voices. At the church door
bellringers practise changes, the harmonics lingering.
The Radio Room is a small stone cottage with a single bed,
a table and chair, oak chest, bathroom, kitchen,
white walls, wood floor, china blue and white.

In the corner is the early telephone equipment
made out of wood and bakelite. This Radio Room
was once the communications centre of the island.
In the white room history's layers unpeel,
time melts. Like light across hilltops,
beacon to beacon, I can throw a thought-line

From this room on Lundy in the Celtic Sea
to my study in Bluff, under Motupohue. The chair is empty,
the computer off. I am not there. Outside lie hills and harbour,
the port going on as usual. Flax and toetoe flattened in the westerly,
a child's bike, macrocarpa, tussock,
cranes, sheds, logs, fuel tanks, sea pewter and silver.

Wake up to lark song over castle ruins. Early sunlight
gilds the courtyard wall. Peaty tarns and granite slabs
flank the road's white-pebbled spine, menhirs couched
in purple and russet heather. The puffin population
has declined, God save the puffins.
The language of this island carries genes of history;

On Eliensis, Annwn, Ynys Gwair, in scalping wind
on a cliff-top above screaming gulls
I stand still thinking backwards, antipodean poet
grafted from ancient taproot in this bedrock,
presently at home among the tussock, lichen, peat-tinged tarns,
cliffs, boulders, ocean of my southern island.

Islands have their spirits. On this cliff path I could meet
a mediaeval saint, a pirate, a 'daring and infatuated ruffian'
or the Barnstaple gentleman who smuggled tobacco
and landed a transport of convicts here for cheap labour
instead of taking them to America, or the last Royalist,
or a Templar, even the mother of King Arthur.

Bedrock holds steady the Old Light. Mauve seed-heads
mourn lichened memorials, Dark Age gravestones
moonscaped by weather, unmoved from this beacon point
since they were carved and placed by someone's hand, right here.
If they spoke what would they say, could I understand
that language at the root of my tongue?

In the Giants' Graves once lay two skeletons, of eight and seven
feet in length. In the porch of St Helen's, the Giant's Pillow
is a granite rectangle, a round depression for his head.
Or else a former druid's altar with a bowl for blood.
Nodes, tunnels, invisible harmonic lines,
scattered flint arrowheads dream up melody.

The dark sentinel castle, Guard of the Fisher King
as like as not, where Perceval saw the Sangreal –
small probability of Perceval beside this shadow-circled pool –
only the sound of a fly, a plicking fish jaw, ripples and splashes
amplified by granite walls. Carp gleam under reflections
of buttercup, clover, small gorse in crevices, honeysuckle,

Familiar bracken, a submerged log, peat water. Shapes
and figures in the granite. A rock and its reflection
make the image of a shield lying on its side.
Who first made these stone steps, this comfortable niche
beside the spring? Who's here besides?
Two ravens on a drystone wall.

The log-book in the Radio Room mentions
the fleeting apparition of a Pygmy Shrew.
Roast Lundy lamb tastes sweet, of wild thyme, peat.
A breeze like a finger strokes my face, touch beyond time.
On the eastern cliff the Templar watches England.
Sheep-tracks cross the heath to Pondsbury, centre of the island.

On the lake there floats a small, reed-covered island,
water vessel in a bowl of sky. Myth tangle-rooted in the rushes,
there's a giant-sized granite Punchbowl as round as a table.
Birds in the rafters of the quiet church. On the lectern lies an
open Bible.
'Too much honey is bad for you, therefore do not seek to win
praise.'
On a pew, a curling photograph of Princess Diana.

St Helen's eight bells bear stern inscriptions:
'I warn that the time has now come for prayers'
'We all sing the praises of God'
'H.G.H, the vicar, had us brought into being'
'Charles Carr & Co. made us A.D.1897'
'When rung confusedly we announce dangers'

'When rung backwards we signify fires'
'When sounding in the right way we proclaim joys'
'I say farewell to the departing souls'
Carved under the clock, TEMPUS SATOR AETERNITATI.
On the 350 million-year-old slate beach
the Celtic Sea rolls to my feet a granite pebble

Circled by a belt of quartz, but for a thin diagonal gap.
When I'm home again I'll make another journey,
imaginary, back to the Island of Honey,
from Motupohue across the sea to the Radio Room.
Ynys Elen will unfold to me complete with cliff paths,
castle ruins, strait church in the fields, lichened

Stone walls, sunlight flooding blood-red heather.
I'll be as unobtrusive as the Pygmy Shrew, revisiting
invisibly, not to disturb a molecule of matter.
The island a green rift in the ocean, tear in space-time,
leaf outlined in white, the single road a spine.
Quartz-gristled granite pebble in my palm, blood-warm.

YOUR EYES

Silver shoals flip
and shirr the calm.
A small ship on the horizon.
The hills bend to the water.

I trust you least in conversation
when you round your eyes
and make your mouth an O
pretending ignorance – not likely –

O you got wicked eyes
that needle me and piss me off, my friend
although I know you're kind to me
and you see deep.

Plain and true
the hills and the horizon.
Your eyes were bright as coal last night,
with grief, when you were speaking of Yvonne.

to Hone 1995

ACKNOWLEDGEMENTS

The manuscript of this book has been completed during my two-year term as Poet Laureate, appointed by the National Library. I am very grateful to the Library for their support.

'Bookworm' and 'Foveaux Express' appeared on the nzepc website.
'Cup Of Tea', 'Our Cow', 'Passion Pantoum', 'Reprise', 'The Hole' and 'Your Eyes' were first published in *Landfall*.
'Etching' was published in *Sport*.
'Notes for Moths' first published with graphic score in Notations 21, ed. Theresa Sauer, a tribute to the composer John Cage (Mark Batty Publisher 2009).
'Photon' was written for Beth Serjeant's anthology 'The Emissary' (forthcoming).
'Ripples' was published in *NZSA Bulletin of New Zealand Studies* No 2.
Poets mentioned are Joanna Paul and Hone Tuwhare.
In the poem 'Wash', 'Zara' refers to a splendid white wine from John Buck's Te Mata Estate.